"Lorene Machado ha[...]
communication gap [...]
never thought I'd see [...]
only get my wife to re[...] ...

—Bob Hope

"Was It Something I Said?"

It's no joke that men and women continue
to speak in foreign languages. Whether
it's about love, sex, food, even doing the
laundry, communicating with the opposite
sex can be a baffling experience.

In this comical, laugh-out-loud gender
handbook, humorist Lorene Machado
confronts head-on the common pitfalls of
male-female communication. Perfect as a
pocket-size translator and uproarious 90s-
style gender dictionary, *Was It Something I
Said?* is an indispensable guide that will clue
you in to what's really being said!

**Lorene Machado lives in Los Angeles and is a
partner in On The Fly Entertainment. She and her
husband, Tony, communicate effortlessly with each
other and their two pit bulls.**

Publisher: W. Quay Hays
Editors: Colby Allerton, Stephen Motika
Art Director: Susan Anson
Designer: Chitra Sekhar
Cover Illustrations: Jeff Wong
Production Director: Trudihope Schlomowitz
Color and PrePress Manager: Bill Castillo
Production Artists: Gaston Moraga, Gus Dawson
Production Assistant: Tom Archibeque

Was It Something I Said?
is published by
General Publishing Group, Inc.
2701 Ocean Park Blvd., Ste. 140
Santa Monica, CA 90405

Comments, suggestions and additions
can be forwarded to the author at
P.O. Box 39952, LA, CA, 90039, or e-mailed to
LOREQ@PRIMENET.COM

Library of Congress Catalog Card Number
96-077592

ISBN 1-57544-000-8

Printed in the USA
10 9 8 7 6 5 4 3 2 1

General Publishing Group
Los Angeles

Dedication:

TO MY PARENTS

Who didn't panic when I was "Class Clown" while my brother

and sister were "Most Likely To Succeed."

And to my husband, Tony, who makes it all make sense.

Introduction:

It was so Los Angeles. Discussing divorce over lunch with a close friend. Actually, she was breaking the news of her separation to me, though I'd of course heard it already from a mutual friend who just couldn't keep her mouth shut. Nonetheless, we both cried into our linguini as the story unfolded. But by the end of the meal, the strangest thing transpired. We were both laughing hysterically. She told me about how the communication had broken down in her marriage, and how they were left to second guess each other all the time. We fantasized about having a "relationship translation guide," and that was the genesis of this book.

Since then, I've bashed brains with a lot of people about this idea and received mountains of feedback and input. And then there are those former "learning experiences" of mine, you know who you are, who provided such great material.

Thanks to my pals who've helped me along the way: Paula Lewis, Suzanne Ali, Rendell and Jennifer, my extended wacky family, the "Dream Team" at Bob Hope Enterprises, Kathleen Madigan, Jon Steingart, The Internet Folk Folks, Merry Aronson, and Raechel Donahue, who slipped the proposal to my publisher, Quay Hays. Also at General Publishing Group, thumbs up to my editor Colby Allerton, and Lori Rick, for making all of the publicity tests "pass/fail." Big wave to Barb Lyon, who's laughed with, and sometimes at, me since my formative years. And special thanks to Caroline Aiken, my southern soul sister, for the quick bond and new direction. Your friendship and music rock my world. Alrighty then.

"Was It Something I Said?"

THE WOMEN

WOMEN ON RELATIONSHIPS

WOMEN ON DRIVING AND CARS

WOMEN ON EATING AND COOKING

WOMEN ON HOME LIFE

WOMAN TO WOMAN

Women on relationships

"If one is lucky, a solitary fantasy can totally transform one million realities."
—*Maya Angelou*

A well-cited magazine article claimed that women over 40-years-old have a better chance of getting killed by a terrorist than of getting married. Some women were shocked by this statistic, while others asked, "what's the catch?"

The exaggerated image of romance that is heaped upon us by television and movies is a fantasy. Music does not swell on cue, and Maui sunsets do not grace every corner of the globe. Consequently, many women are throwing away their dream of meeting Mr. Right and setting their sights on Mr. Good Enough.

<u>If a woman says:</u>

I'm fine.

<u>It means:</u>

I'm about to have a nervous breakdown of colossal proportions.

If a woman says:

I'm on my period.

It means:

*I wouldn't sleep with you
on a dare.*

If a woman says:

I'm just not attracted to
you anymore.

It means:

Is your brother single?

If a woman says:

This is my first time.

It means:

This is my first time with you.

>—·—>—◦—<—·—<

If a woman says:

We need to talk.

It means:

How quickly can you pack?

I didn't hear the phone ring.

I always unplug the phone when I'm having sex.

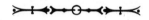

I think you're getting a little too attached to me.

The FBI Witness Relocation Plan is starting to sound really appealing.

If a woman says:

You're not my type.

It means:

You're not filthy rich.

If a woman says:

I don't sleep with men on the first date.

It means:

I don't sleep with anyone who only tips ten percent.

If a woman says:

We need to communicate better.

It means:

I'm always right and you're always wrong, so you might as well learn to live with it.

I've never had a relationship
that's worked out.

*I am a black hole
of dysfunction.*

I love you like a brother.

*I hate my brother, and I'd
never go out with you in a
million years.*

Do you want to come in
for a drink?

*Do you want to come in
for sex?*

I'm not a morning person.

*OK, I'll sleep with you, but
I'm not cooking breakfast.*

No one has made me feel like this before.

The ceiling should be painted beige.

I'm just not ready for a commitment.

I'm a slut.

You know what you did.

My old boyfriend was a jerk, and I'm going to blame you for everything he ever did to me.

I'm just about ready to go.

*I'm only going to change
three more times before
we leave.*

Of course I don't mind if you
smoke.

*Personally, I don't mind if
you burst into flames.*

Women on driving and cars

> *"A 'woman driver' is one who drives like a man and gets blamed for it."*
> —*Patricia Ledger*
> National Junior Commerce Drivers Ability test winner

Ask any couple where the majority of their fights occur, and most of them will say "in the car." Many men believe that the "Y" chromosome endows them with the driving skills of Mario Andretti and that women drivers turn the streets into a real-life version of Mr. Toad's Wild Ride.

On the other hand, women think that men are, well, basically trying to kill them every time they get behind the wheel. It's true that no woman has ever won the Indianapolis 500, but that doesn't really mean anything. No man has ever won an Olympic Gold medal in synchronized swimming, and women aren't saying that men are lousy at that.

If he insists on driving, here are some suggestions for reducing auto altercations:

- Walk
- Close your eyes
- Install a state-of-the-art stereo system

Remember, you are not alone.

Shouldn't we stop and ask for directions?

I'm curious to find out if we're in the same hemisphere as our destination.

Are we going to take the shortcut again?

It means:

I hope this party is dull because we're gonna miss it.

If a woman says:

Gee, what a nice car.

It means:

At least there's no possibility of car-jacking on this date.

What a quaint little
roadside cafe.

I have to go to the bathroom.

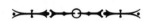

Don't you think you're
following that car a little
too closely?

*We left home with one car
and I don't want to return
with two.*

Do you mind if I drive?

*You're too drunk to drive
and I want to live to
never see you again.*

If a woman says:

No honey, I think you're a
fine driver.

It means:

*I can't wait until this Valium
kicks in.*

If a woman says:

We should buy this car. It
has low mileage and it
handles great.

It means:

I like the color.

My husband checked this car out thoroughly, and it looks like a good deal.

It means:

He kicked the tires and we're broke.

If a woman says:

My mechanic is so great. He only charged me $600.00 to fix my brakes.

It means:

I needed brake fluid.

Dirt protects the car's paint.

My car is a roving trash heap.

I wash my car twice a week.

But I won't change my oil until I smell serious smoke.

If a woman says:

This is my favorite song.

It means:

If I turn the volume up, I don't have to listen to my brakes squeak.

If a woman says:

How's your driving record?

It means:

You make Apollo 13 look like a joy ride.

Why don't you just let me drive in peace?

*I thought that stop
signs were optional
if there are
no cops around;
so sue me.*

Women on eating and cooking

"Can you imagine a world without men? No crime and lots of happy, fat women."
—*Marion Smith*

Every day some genius comes up with a new form of torture for women to achieve the ultimate goal—anorexia. Just as another diet doctor falls victim to foul play, someone like Jenny Craig appears on the horizon. As a result, women spend their days dieting, aerobicizing, and lipo-sucking to within an inch of their lives. Anyone who believes that women are less adept at math than men has never seen a dieting woman calculate the calories to inches-on-your-thighs equation.

Cooking can be a nightmare, too. Being the proud owner of two X-chromosomes doesn't necessarily produce a Martha Stewart. In the kitchen, most women simply improvise to impress. There, I said it.

The reward for this relentless work? Usually, it's the sweet sound of your loving boyfriend or husband saying those three magic words, "You're gaining weight."

I can eat and eat and eat,
and I never gain a pound.

It means:

I have no friends.

If a woman says:

I'm not hungry.

It means:

I'm about to die of starvation, so let's eat. Besides, I can always throw up afterwards.

If a woman says:

I've been eating nothing but
vegetables every day.

It means:

*And nothing but cheesecake
every night.*

If a woman says:

I'm just going to have
a salad.

It means:

*My freezer is full of
Haagen Dazs.*

Can I choose the restaurant tonight?

I'm tired of eating at restaurants that use plastic utensils.

I'm saving room for dessert.

It means:

In fact, I'm thinking of building on an addition for it.

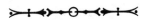

If a woman says:

I'm on a very restricted diet.

It means:

I restrict my eating to when no one else is around.

Should we flip those burgers now?

I got the crowbar from the garage.

>—+—◦—+—<

Let's just have another beer before we bring the steaks out.

Bob lit his hair on fire with the charcoal lighter.

Aren't those flames a
little high?

*Will those burgers be
done by the time the
firemen arrive?*

Do you want some ice cream?

I want some ice cream.

Boy, this skirt really shrunk
in the dryer, didn't it?

Do I look fat?

Don't come into the kitchen. This is a delicate dish.

I don't want you to see the empty Byrds Eye boxes on the counter.

I'm a vegetarian.

I'm broke.

>—!—‹›—⊙—‹›—!—‹

I make the best clam chowder
you've ever tasted.

*I have a can opener and
a microwave.*

Women on home life

"The strength of a nation is derived from the integrity of its homes."

—*Confucius*

The irony of the words on my mom's favorite apron eluded me as a child: "To Hell with Housework." Fact is, I never really saw my mother do much housework, but my childhood home was always immaculate. I, her oldest daughter, did not inherit that knack for cleaning. Neither did a lot of my female friends. Maybe, in a subconscious way, we're fighting back with inaction and apathy where our mothers fought back with aprons. We're here! We're slobs! Get over it!

In the '90s, where both partners in a relationship are usually working professionally, the lines between household duties are starting to blur. And that's where the fun begins.

Are you sure you know
how to fix this?

*Oh well, it's only a family
heirloom. At least I have
a boyfriend.*

What show are you looking for?

I hope I have enough double-A batteries to fuel that remote control.

No, I haven't seen your blue tank top.

Not since I used it to clean the toilet.

><+>·+<>·+<+><

We should do some laundry.

I just maxed out all my credit cards buying new clothes.

Look honey, IKEA is having a sale.

I'd like to have furniture that doesn't include milk crates for once in my life.

I'll wash the dishes
if you cook.

*I'll figure out a way to
get him to wash the
dishes AFTER I eat.*

A little dust never killed anyone.

The dust bunnies have bred into a frenzy.

Have you seen the dog lately?

I think the lawn in the backyard needs to be mowed.

We should put some
time aside to work on
the house.

*You should put some
time aside to work on
the house.*

Oh great, another do-it-yourself home project.

I hope I saved the number for that general contractor we used last time.

Woman to woman

"Some of us are becoming the men we want to marry."

—*Gloria Steinem*

Women can usually count on other women to tell them the truth, unless it's a salesperson at Macy's, in which case you'll find that everything looks good on you.

Women have honed the skill of being direct with each other without saying the words. It's an unspoken yet impressive skill, much like birds in flight who navigate in tandem. The mystery of why women who work in the same office together tend to "cycle" together cannot be explained by modern science. The bottom line is that women are simply in sync with each other.

But every once in awhile, a bird will stray or, God forbid, someone will skip her period. Hence, there may be times when you're not so sure how to interpret a comment from your gal pal, in which case, you may want to refer to this chapter.

I'm sorry to call you so late at night.

I'm really depressed, and the mall is closed.

I just bought the cutest blouse on sale.

Do you know anything about mortgaging houses?

If a woman says:

We have an open relationship.

It means:

Divorce is too expensive and inconvenient so we sleep around.

We'll be friends for life.

I don't think your boyfriend is cute at all.

>—┼—◇—O—◇—┼—<

Don't dress up, it's casual.

I'm wearing a bustier and heels.

He loves me for my mind.

Besides that, he has no faults.

> ⟩—⟨⟩—◯—⟨⟩—⟨

Ugh, I can't believe you're going out with him.

I've always wanted to go out with him.

If a woman says:

He reminds me a lot of my ex-husband.

It means:

Dump him quick.

If a woman says:

He has one of the great minds of the century.

It means:

The 16th century.

You look great.

Last time I saw you, you looked like hell.

You've lost weight, haven't you?

Good, I still weigh less than you do.

If a woman says:

We've been broken up for a long time, go ahead and date him.

It means:

Let's see how you deal with a man who insists on wearing a lampshade during sex.

He's not sleazy. He's just different.

I worship the ground he slithers on.

My hair is naturally auburn.

Once it is dyed.

She's so materialistic. I'd never want to be like her.

I'd give anything to drive her Mercedes.

We went out a couple of
times. It was nothing
serious.

*I still can't get the
blueberry stains out of
my sheets.*

Someday we'll laugh
about this.

*But for right now, I would
suggest revenge.*

I promise I won't tell anyone.

Until after you leave.

I was hoping he'd change.

Into James Bond.

That haircut makes you look
like Meryl Streep.

In "Sophie's Choice."

You look good in
that color.

It means:

*Yellow brings out the
sallow in your skin.*

We weren't gossiping. We were talking.

We were gossiping.

After he made dinner, we redecorated my apartment.

He's the nicest gay man I've ever dated.

"Was It Something I Said?"

It's no joke that men and women continue to speak in foreign languages. Whether it's about love, sex, food, even doing the laundry, communicating with the opposite sex can be a baffling experience.

In this comical, laugh-out-loud gender handbook, humorist Lorene Machado confronts head-on the common pitfalls of male-female communication. Perfect as a pocket-size translator and uproarious 90s-style gender dictionary, *Was It Something I Said?* is an indispensable guide that will clue you in to what's really being said!

Lorene Machado lives in Los Angeles and is a partner in On The Fly Entertainment. She and her husband, Tony, communicate effortlessly with each other and their two pit bulls.

Publisher: W. Quay Hays
Editors: Colby Allerton, Stephen Motika
Art Director: Susan Anson
Designer: Chitra Sekhar
Cover Illustrations: Jeff Wong
Production Director: Trudihope Schlomowitz
Color and PrePress Manager: Bill Castillo
Production Artists: Gaston Moraga, Gus Dawson
Production Assistant: Tom Archibeque

Was It Something I Said?
is published by
General Publishing Group, Inc.
2701 Ocean Park Blvd., Ste. 140
Santa Monica, CA 90405

Comments, suggestions and additions
can be forwarded to the author at
P.O. Box 39952, LA, CA, 90039, or e-mailed to
LOREQ@PRIMENET.COM

Library of Congress Catalog Card Number
96-077592

ISBN 1-57544-000-8

Printed in the USA
10 9 8 7 6 5 4 3 2 1

General Publishing Group
Los Angeles

Dedication:

TO MY PARENTS

Who didn't panic when I was "Class Clown" while my brother

and sister were "Most Likely To Succeed."

And to my husband, Tony, who makes it all make sense.

Introduction:

It was so Los Angeles. Discussing divorce over lunch with a close friend. Actually, she was breaking the news of her separation to me, though I'd of course heard it already from a mutual friend who just couldn't keep her mouth shut. Nonetheless, we both cried into our linguini as the story unfolded. But by the end of the meal, the strangest thing transpired. We were both laughing hysterically. She told me about how the communication had broken down in her marriage, and how they were left to second guess each other all the time. We fantasized about having a "relationship translation guide," and that was the genesis of this book.

Since then, I've bashed brains with a lot of people about this idea and received mountains of feedback and input. And then there are those former "learning experiences" of mine, you know who you are, who provided such great material.

Thanks to my pals who've helped me along the way: Paula Lewis, Suzanne Ali, Rendell and Jennifer, my extended wacky family, the "Dream Team" at Bob Hope Enterprises, Kathleen Madigan, Jon Steingart, The Internet Folk Folks, Merry Aronson, and Raechel Donahue, who slipped the proposal to my publisher, Quay Hays. Also at General Publishing Group, thumbs up to my editor Colby Allerton, and Lori Rick, for making all of the publicity tests "pass/fail." Big wave to Barb Lyon, who's laughed with, and sometimes at, me since my formative years. And special thanks to Caroline Aiken, my southern soul sister, for the quick bond and new direction. Your friendship and music rock my world. Alrighty then.

"Was It Something I Said?"

THE MEN

MEN ON RELATIONSHIPS

MEN ON FAMILY

MEN ON HOME LIFE

MEN ON COMPUTERS AND THE INTERNET

MAN TO MAN

Men on relationships

"The great question...which I have not been able to answer, despite my thirty years of research into the feminine soul, is 'What does a woman want?'"

—*Sigmund Freud*

Men truly do not have a clue as to what women want in a relationship, and women are still conferring with each other to come up with an answer. The bottom line is that what women want is a complex issue, with no obvious answer.

Men are so much easier.

The myth persists that men are only interested in sex. This is close, but not entirely true. They like to eat, too. But if a man were to weigh the options, he'd surely rather let his stomach rumble a little rather than risk missing the next orgasm. This is not to say that men are a lost cause. Sometimes it's simply the glint off a woman's hair, the sparkle in her eyes, or the way that she agrees with everything he says that makes a man fall in love. Then it's back to reality, and he's imagining what she looks like naked.

I love you.

I want to sleep with you.

> ⟩—⟨⟩—☉—⟨⟩—⟨

I'll call you.

You'll never hear from me again.

The thought of a long-term relationship doesn't appeal to me.

I'm ready to have sex with someone else now.

Are you OK?

Are you on your period?

>—<•>—<O>—<•>—<

I just want to be friends.

*Your best friend is
really cute.*

She's got a great personality.

Lassie go home.

> ⊶—◦—⊷

Without you, my life has
no meaning.

*Is this a good time to tell you
about my history of stalking?*

My place is a mess. Can we meet at your house?

I live with my parents.

———— ❦ ————

I lost your phone number.

I washed my hands.

I've always been kind of shy.

I have no personality. Do you mind if I borrow yours?

><+>-○-<+><

I'm a '90s kind of guy. I think we should go dutch.

I'm unemployed.

I brought you flowers because I'm crazy about you.

I'm having an affair.

><+>+O+<+><

I'll be back soon.

I'll be back after last call.

If a man says:

I'll still respect you in the morning.

It means:

I promise to drive you back to your car in the morning.

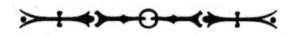

If a man says:

What's your sign?

It means:

What's your phone number?

Size doesn't matter.

Do the words "little smokie" mean anything to you?

I'm monogamous.

I've never had a threesome.

I lost track of time.

Although I was fully aware of the time, I was having more fun with my friends than I would have been having with you.

I'm between jobs.

My last two girlfriends supported me. Do you have a problem with that?

>—⟨◆⟩—●—⟨◆⟩—⟨

Can we see each other again?

I still have five spaces free on my speed dialer.

If a man says:

Yes, dear.

It means:

Maybe if I agree with her, she'll stop talking.

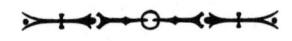

If a man says:

I read *Playboy* for the articles.

It means:

I read the phone book for the pictures.

We've both changed.

And I'm cashing out.

My life is an open book.

—of fiction.

I like the way you think...

*I'm the greatest man
on earth.*

><+>·O·<+><

I'm getting in touch with
my inner child.

*You look like an airhead,
and I think this will
appeal to you.*

We should spend more time together, just the two of us.

Your neurotic friends are driving me crazy.

I only do drugs recreationally.

I can't afford to do drugs all the time.

I've been meaning to call you.

Jim says you put out.

>─┼─❖─❖─O─❖─┼─<

I just found your phone number.

Bill says you put out.

>─┼─❖─❖─O─❖─┼─<

I was too shy to call until now.

Everyone says you put out.

Men on family

"Happiness is having a large, loving, caring, close-knit family in another city."
—*George Burns*

Meeting your girlfriend's or wife's family is extremely enlightening. It helps you realize that those annoying little habits are not unique to your partner; they were actually bred into her. It makes you think twice about having children.

Chances are that your family is no Walton's clone either. But what good is a family if it doesn't embarrass the hell out of you from time to time? They're only doing their job.

No matter how crazy or dysfunctional our families may be, we love them. It's best for partners to come up with an agreement, something along the lines of "I'll endure yours if you'll endure mine." And on those occasions when we're riding out the family roller coaster, we usually don't realize until later that we're actually having a good time.

If a man says:

I can't wait to take you home to meet my family.

It means:

I'm too chicken to break up with you, and this always works.

You look a lot like your cousins.

Your gene pool makes Britain's royal family look like the United Colors of Benetton.

How fun, your family is having another reunion.

Why can't you be like normal families and just get together when someone dies or gets married?

Of course I don't mind if your mother stays with us for a couple of days.

Hello Ramada? What's your nightly rate?

>—⟨⟩—O—⟨⟩—⟨

Your parents are family; they can never overstay their welcome.

If they don't leave soon, I'm gonna charge rent.

Where should we spend the holidays this year?

Who do you think is going to cook the best food and give the best presents this year?

I'm getting old.

I used to bring drugs to family gatherings and now I bring cameras.

>—⊙—⦿—⊙—⦿—<

You're not marrying my family, you're marrying me.

Okay, they live in the same town, but it's not like they'll be sleeping over every night.

Don't be silly, I'm crazy about your kids.

I'll find a way to ditch the little Demon Seeds at a gas station restroom if it's the last thing I do.

My little brother is coming to visit tomorrow.

Hey, at least I'm giving you a day to drink the beer and hide the checkbook.

My family is really close.

That incident with the near-murder of my last girlfriend really brought us together.

Your father is a cool guy.

Your father has the most complete dirty magazine collection I've ever seen.

Men on home life

"Sometimes I wonder if men and women suit each other. Perhaps they should live next door and just visit now and then."
—Katharine Hepburn

Men doing housework is appealing and sexy. Look at the success of Mrs. Doubtfire. It wasn't even Robin Williams' best performance, yet it was a big hit. When Mrs. Doubtfire wielded her Hoover, it fulfilled the fantasy of the average housewife. A man who could cook and clean, not always well, but always with enthusiasm and commitment. Sure, he was wearing a dress, but who pays attention to little details these days?

Now, if they ever got Tootsie (a girl's best friend and a great listener) and Mrs. Doubtfire together for a movie... Excuse me, I have to get my agent on the phone...

<u>If a man says:</u>

I'll fix it.

<u>It means:</u>

Buy a new one.

All that toaster needs
is a new plug and it will
work fine.

*I'll put it in the pile with
the other things that just
need new plugs.*

Football season starts tomorrow.

*See you after
Super Bowl Sunday.*

I got you some new
doll clothes.

I did the laundry.

I was thinking, you look
really good in pink.

I did the laundry.

Why don't we go shopping for a new sweater for you?

I did the laundry.

I know I put my keys
right here on the table.

*The keys are on
the counter.*

You should look before you sit on the toilet. It's not my fault I left the seat up and you fell through.

I want to sleep on the couch.

I have a headache.

The final four is on TV tonight.

>—<+>—O—<+>—<

I finally found a good use for your antique bowl.

I just changed the oil in my car.

41

A woman's place is
in the kitchen.

*I'm ready to live
alone again.*

I think we should buy this house. It's a fixer-upper.

By the time we fix this house, we will have spent twice the asking price.

If we do it ourselves, we'll save money.

Until we have to pay a contractor to come in and rebuild our custom home.

>—‹+›—⊙—‹+›—‹

C'mon it'll be fun, it's something we can do together.

We'll be fighting by the time we get the first roll of wallpaper up.

I don't have the right tool for that.

I have no idea how to fix that.

———◦———

I was going to get to that tomorrow.

I have 24 hours to think up another excuse.

Men on computers and the Internet

"The computer is only a fast idiot, it has no imagination; it cannot originate action. It is, and will remain, only a tool to man."

—*American Library*

Association statement on Univac computer exhibited at New York World's Fair 1964

The term "better than sliced bread" might be true for the first time with the explosion of the personal computer and the Internet. This incredible network was designed to shuttle scientific information around the globe and to serve as an indestructible means of communication in the event of a nuclear war. Two noble objectives. In a glowing example of the human spirit, it was perhaps inevitable that someone would find a way to have sex on it.

However, the information superhighway offers a wealth of information beyond the infamous pornography news groups and the s&m chat rooms. One can read the daily news, keep up with stocks, and even share fishing tips with people from Iceland. Of course, some men are so caught up with the technology of computers that they would choose a high baud over a hot bod. These guys are forces to be reckoned with, and we pretty much have Bill Gates to thank for it.

It's certainly no secret that the information superhighway may be the world's most sophisticated dating service. The Internet levels the playing field in relationships and is changing the way the sexes interact with each other. The written word rules and safe sex has a whole new meaning. The phrase, "you're not my type," can now be taken literally. But even in this wacky new playing arena, there's always a chance for love at first byte.

I just upgraded to two gigs and now I'm saving up for more ram and a 19-inch, non-interlaced, high resolution monitor.

It means:

I'm a virgin.

If a man says:

I think I'll rewrite that report; it was too wordy anyhow.

It means:

I deleted my file.

>—•—<

If a man says:

Your note must have gotten lost.

It means:

Your note must have gotten lost in my "trash" mailbox.

Oh, it's great to cyber-chat with you again. How are your kids?

It means:

20 million people on the internet and I still can't find someone who'll talk dirty with me.

What's your e-mail address?

I met my last girlfriend on the internet.

>—<>—<—<>—<

I'm tall, dark, and handsome.

I'm puny, pale, and pimply.

Let's meet in person
sometime.

God, I hope you're a woman.

———◦———

My name is Fred, but you
can call me "The Viper."

I'm the global village idiot.

Our relationship wasn't going anywhere.

She left me for a man with a faster modem.

I only use my internet account for e-mail.

I prefer phone sex over computer sex.

My modem cut us off.

It was getting too hard to type with one hand.

I really hope to get married someday.

I'd really like to have sex without my computer someday.

I haven't been on-line lately.

I've been logging on under another user name.

My computer has been down.

My on-line fling dumped me.

Man to man

> *"It is one of the blessings of old friends that you can afford to be stupid with them."*
> —*Ralph Waldo Emerson*

It's been said that women are prone to self-deprecation, while men are prone to self-worship. Perhaps this is because, physically, men have a little more leeway. Think of a famous sexy woman and names like Sharon Stone and Demi Moore come to mind. A list of famous sexy men could contain names as diverse as Alec Baldwin to Woody Allen. We have sexy male nerds, but no sexy female nerds (OK, there's Lisa Loeb, but that's another story).

Men love men. I'm not talking about in a sexual way, though that's all right too, but in a real Bud Light "I love you, man" sort of way. Male bonding is real. Guys stick up for each other and cover for each other. That's why they're never wrong. They're too busy agreeing with each other.

Bottom line: Women may never love men as much as men love themselves.

She's very intelligent.

I dumped her.

><+>-⊙-<+><

She's a tramp.

She dumped me.

She's kind of shallow.

*She didn't talk about
me enough.*

>—‹•›—O—‹•›—‹

Any woman in this room would want me...

...to go away.

I'm hungry.

I'm awake.

I'm horny.

I'm awake.

If a man says:

We don't have that much in common.

It means:

She reads books.

>─┤─◆─○─◆─├─<

If a man says:

We're just friends.

It means:

She won't return my calls.

She was getting too serious.

*I asked her to marry me and
she broke up with me.*

>—⟨•⟩—⟨•⟩—⟨

She's great. She has a great
sense of humor, lots of cool
friends, and knows more
about sports than I do.

I'm dating a lesbian.

I'm gonna make six figures
this year.

*Including the decimal point,
of course.*

I was accepted to Harvard,
Yale, and Princeton.

I have my G.E.D.

Money is no object to me.

I have no money.

❖ ◆ ◦ ◆ ❖

I hate to brag, but I do pretty well for myself.

I'm really good at sponging off of other people.

We were going to go out last night, but I was really tired.

She stood me up.

I used to be a great
rebounder before I blew my
knee out.

*I was a benchwarmer
without equal.*

>⟶⟨⟩⟶⊙⟵⟨⟩⟵<

I'm glad you two broke up.
You weren't right for
each other.

I hope her number is listed.